A Spark of Hope

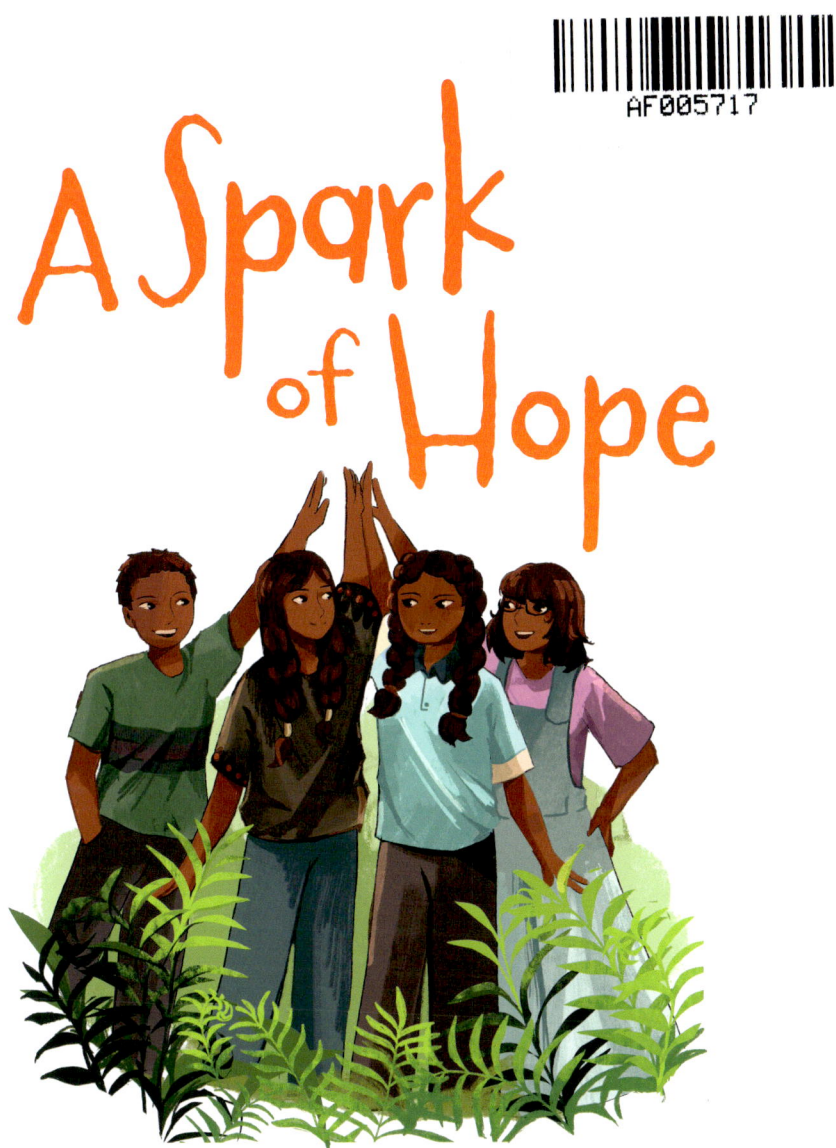

Written by Fiona Barker
Illustrated by Jade van der Zalm

Collins

Chapter 1

Hope lived with her Pa in the forest. She had lots of friends and loved her life among the trees and wildlife.

But Hope still felt like there was something missing.

All her friends knew what they wanted in life.

Kenna had always been interested in bodies and figuring out how they worked. Hope remembered when Kenna had cut her finger once when she was helping her mother prepare fish for smoking. Kenna had drawn pictures of what the wound looked like every day as it mended.

"Isn't that a bit gross?" Hope asked.

"No, it's so fascinating!" said Kenna. "I need to see how things heal. It'll help when I'm a doctor. I'll know how to fix people."

Fia was clever and good at explaining things. Their teacher, Mrs McIntyre, was always setting them tricky homework. If anyone had a question, Fia was the one they went to for the answers.

"You'd be a great teacher," stated Hope.

"Thanks," smiled Fia. "That's what I'd like to do one day."

On the way to school, they'd all stop in at Ishkode's garden to help him feed the collection of animals he was caring for. People from all over the place brought him orphaned raccoons and birds with broken wings. He had once even looked after a porcupine with a cracked tooth. That had been a prickly customer! There was always something different.

"I'm going be a vet like my big brother," said Ishkode.

But Hope didn't know what she wanted to do. She felt small in a huge world. How could her one voice make a difference to anything? She could see that all her friends had fire in their hearts. But she just didn't feel the same spark. Not yet.

Chapter 2

Hope hardly had time to think about the future anyway. She was busy every day helping her Pa.

In the autumn, cold winds blew in from the North and promised snow. Hope helped Pa with chopping and stacking wood.

"Help me take the branches off this tree that's come down in the winds," puffed Pa. "Then we can cut it and add it to the store."

They worked together, cheeks flushed with cold and effort, to build towering stacks that would see them through winter.

Splinters were a problem when working with wood, but Kenna was always happy to help.

"I'll sort that out for you, Hope," she said.

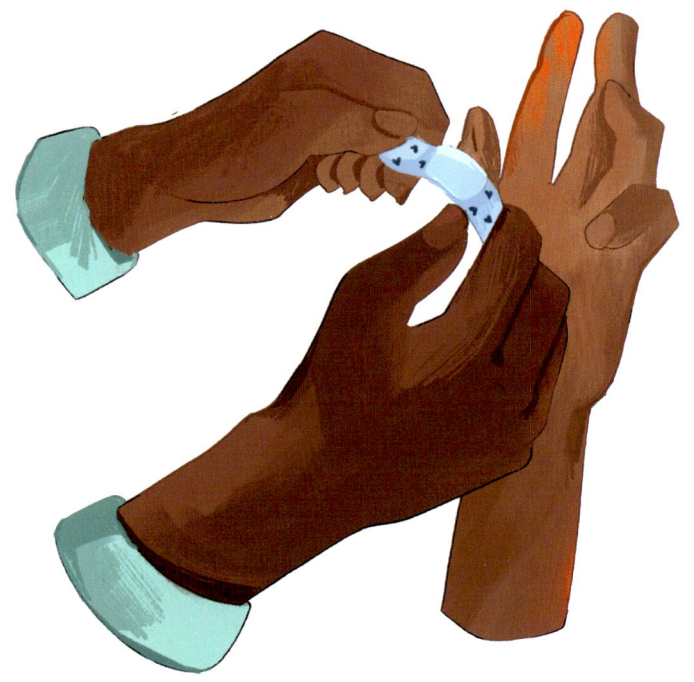

"Look at the rings on this one," said Fia. "It's like reading the tree's life story. Look, you can see each spring growth. The wider rings are where it was an easy year with good weather and the narrow rings show where the winter was really hard."

Hope helped Ishkode choose a twisted offcut for his newest patient. Someone had brought him a young squirrel with half its tail missing. It would love to run up and down the branch once it had healed and got its balance back.

Chapter 3

When the snow finally came in winter, it wrapped the forest in a thick, soft blanket. Hope and her friends had to keep the paths clear with snow shovels so they could easily get fresh logs from the store. Winter was hard work! Usually, though, Hope would have a bit of time left at the end of the day before the low sun finally set. That's when she would creep into the quiet of the frozen forest on her own. If she was lucky, she might catch a glimpse of a snowshoe hare. She held her breath as one hopped silently across the snow, marvelling at its winter whiteness.

In spring, the light stretched into the evenings again. On their way home from school, Hope and her friends searched for the first signs of baby hares.

"Look how that bush has been nibbled, just around the base, low to the ground," whispered Kenna.

"Tracks!" pointed Fia. "See how small that second set is compared to the big ones."

"Yes, but the hares are fast," breathed Ishkode. "They're born to run."

"Their feet make them silent too. It's just like they're wearing slippers," said Hope. She longed to see more than just clues, but she knew the mother hare was too clever and kept her babies well hidden.

Chapter 4

In the mornings, the friends stopped at Ishkode's house to check on the progress of his new patient: a beaver with a damaged leg. Then they ran to school together through lush bracken. It seemed to appear from nowhere under the trees, unrolling its leafy fronds to rustle in the spring breeze. Suddenly everything was green.

Spring flew by in a whirl of new life. Fish jumped in the lakes, flowers bloomed and the sky was alive with birds and insects.

But all too soon, it seemed like summer was racing towards them again. Already the curling bracken was crisp and brown.

"The bracken is dry so early," said Pa, shaking his head. "It's going to be another hot summer."

There had always been fires. Sometimes they were started by the lightning of a summer storm. But other times, Pa would read the newspaper and shake his head.

"Another fire," he said. "It says here they think it was a discarded match this time. Last week it was a barbeque someone had left behind. They just don't think. Or maybe they don't care."

Pa sighed.

"Some people don't deserve to come here," Hope declared.

"But it's not only that," said Pa. "The ground is drying out sooner each year, too."

Hope saw on the news that things were changing all over the world. Scientists were recording changes in the temperature and the weather.

But she also saw the changes right outside her home. The bracken was curled and crisp before the end of spring. It seemed the fire came earlier every summer.

Chapter 5

Hope remembered how one fire had nearly reached their home last year. It had seemed as though it was a living thing with a mind of its own. Hope could still hear the snap as it smacked its lips and licked at the leaves in the forest, ever hungry. Pa had been clever though. He worked to clear an area around the house, pulling out scrubby bushes and weeds.

"The flames won't be able to jump the gap," he had said.

Hope trusted Pa but it hadn't stopped her feeling worried.

And they had been lucky. Late in the afternoon, dark clouds had gathered over the forest and a sudden thunderstorm had brought rain. Hope remembered how the fire had hissed and slunk away, sulkily.

But there was no sign of rain now. The sun of a new summer beat down and woke another fiery dragon. At first, it nibbled at the edges of the forest: tasting, curious, hungry.

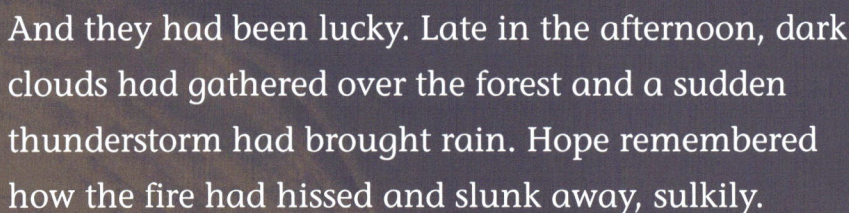

Hope heard the crackle of burning grass and dried leaves. She was afraid but she knew she had to do something. She had to act.

"I need to warn everyone," she cried and ran back into the house.

Chapter 6

Hope phoned her friends.

"The dragon is coming again, Kenna."

"Get ready, Fia."

"Make sure the animals are safe, Ishkode."

As the sun rose in the sky, it grew hotter and hotter. In the furious heat, the dragon roared. It began to consume the forest, tree by tree, leaving only blackened stumps behind it. It crept closer, closer to the houses of Hope and her friends.

Hope felt the breath of the dragon hot on her cheeks. Fear prickled down her back as she wondered what else she could do.

Ahead of the beast, the air was alight with embers and sparks. On a dark winter's night, around a bonfire with marshmallows, it would have been pretty.
But this was the dragon's breath, bringing only danger.

"Take the pipe, Hope, and dampen down the roof," said Pa, passing her the hose. "We need to soak it so the embers can't catch hold."

With each glowing, half-burned leaf that landed, Hope's heart beat faster. Her chest burned like a dry branch caught in the flames.

Chapter 7

It was then that the hare appeared. It bolted out of the forest, running from the dragon.

Its brown summer fur was singed and smoking.

Its nose was sore from the heat.

Its sides were heaving with the effort of escape.

The hare flopped at Hope's feet and looked up at her with eyes that reflected the amber of the flames. For one long moment, it seemed like the whole world was there with Hope and the hare.

And in that moment, Hope felt the wind change. She heard the dragon give a final angry roar before it was pulled down the valley and away. Pa sat down for the first time in days, exhausted but grateful. But Hope wasn't relieved.

She was angry.

Angry that she had to face this every summer.

Angry for the hare that had lost its home.

The fire had gone for now, but it had left a spark inside her.

Chapter 8

Hope fought for the hare.

The summer heat hung heavy in the air. The awful smell of the now distant dragon lingered on. It stung the back of Hope's throat. But now she had something else to focus on. She made a makeshift bed for the hare in a box and gently stroked an unburned patch of fur as she watched its chest rise and fall.

"Hang on, little one. You're safe now," she whispered.

Kenna arrived, bringing a flask with her.

"Here," she said.

"It can't drink out of that," said Hope.

"This is for you," said Kenna. "You need to look after yourself if you want to look after the hare."

Fia arrived next. She took out her notebook.

"I did some research and checked what hares need to help them recover. It'll be difficult but we can do it. It needs water. And we'll need to get something to soothe its skin where it's sore from the heat."

"I can help with that," said Ishkode. "My brother gave me this ointment. We need to gently clean the wounds and then put this on. I've brought a water dropper, too, to help it drink something."

Kenna took charge of the water, letting the hare drink just a little at a time. Hope and Fia gently bathed its burns and Ishkode whispered gently to it as he applied the soothing cream his brother had given him.

"I know it's going to be hard," said Hope. "But we have to try. This hare could have run anywhere but it came to me. I have to give it a chance. I can't give up on it now."

Chapter 9

When the friends had done all they could, Hope watched as the hare's breathing calmed. Eventually, with a last look at Hope, it let its eyes flutter closed and it fell asleep in the box.

"We've done all we can for the time being," said Kenna, "Now it's up to the hare. You should get some rest, Hope. It might be a long night."

Hope kept watch beside the hare that night. Pa brought her drinks and snacks. Eventually, just as the sun peeped over the horizon casting a grey light through the remaining trees, Hope fell asleep.

She dreamed of dragons and flame-filled forests.

Chapter 10

Hope woke with a start as Kenna gently shook her shoulder.

"We came to see how your hare is doing," she said.

The hare! *Her* hare! How could she have fallen asleep?

Hope gently lifted the blanket she had placed over her patient. At first it seemed there was no movement and Hope felt her heart turn over in her chest.

But then, with a twitch of its cream-covered nose, the hare stretched and opened its eyes. Fia had left some fresh clover inside the box and now the hare reached over to sniff it.

"Look! It's eating!" smiled Ishkode. "That's so amazing, Hope. If it's eating, it means it's getting better."

Chapter 11

Over the next few days, the friends took turns caring for the hare. Hope spent hours talking softly to it. As she watched the hare fight back after the fire, the spark in Hope's heart grew into a flame of promise for the future.

On the third morning, the hare sat up for the first time and looked boldly at Hope.

"It's healing so quickly," said Kenna.

"I've made a note of everything we did in case it helps someone else save a hare one day," said Fia proudly.

Ishkode knelt down beside the hare and spoke softly. "Hey there, little one. Hope was right. You're going to be OK. You'll soon be hopping around in the forest again."

The hare gained strength quickly and soon the friends gathered to say goodbye. As the yellow of summer turned to the oranges, browns and russet reds of autumn, they knew the time was right. As they walked through the woods, new life burst from around the blackened tree stumps. Green shoots pushed through the soil and fresh leaves unfolded.

"Look how things are regrowing already," said Fia.

Eventually they reached an area of undamaged forest and let the hare go. It lifted its nose to the breeze, flicked its black-tipped ears, looked back at Hope for a moment and bounded away into the trees.

Chapter 12

And that was where Hope's fight really began.

"We did it. We really did it," smiled Hope.

"You did it, Hope," said Kenna. "You believed in the hare when it couldn't fight for itself."

The hare had no voice, but Hope did. The anger still burned inside her and made her determined. Determined to do something. Now Hope knew what she wanted to do. A passion had been ignited. Kenna wanted to look after people. Fia wanted to teach. Ishkode wanted to care for animals. Hope wanted to give a voice to the voiceless. She wanted to speak for animals, for people, for places that couldn't speak for themselves. She had fought for the hare and now she would fight for the forest.

Hope worked hard to learn why her forest home was catching fire more often. By talking to anyone who would listen, Hope found more friends to help in her fight. Other people were angry, too, and Hope learned to use her voice to fan the flames of anger into action.

Together, they fought for the forest. They fought for the sea, the sky and the earth.

And, with Hope, they knew they had a chance.

A voice for the voiceless

Ideas for reading

Written by Gill Matthews
Primary Literacy Consultant

Reading objectives:
- make inferences on the basis of what is being said and done
- predict what might happen on the basis of what has been read so far
- explain and discuss their understanding of books, poems and other material, both those that they listen to and those that they read for themselves

Spoken language objectives:
- articulate and justify answers, arguments and opinions
- use spoken language to develop understanding through speculating, hypothesising, imagining and exploring ideas
- participate in discussions, presentations, performances, role play, improvisations and debates

Curriculum links: Science: Living things and their habitats

Word count: 2433

Interest words: determined, passion, ignited

Resources: ICT for research, paper and pens

Build a context for reading

- Ask children to look closely at the front cover of the book and to read the title.
- Explore what the title means to them.
- Discuss what children can see on the cover. What do they think is happening?
- Read the back cover blurb. Encourage children to predict what might happen in the story.

Understand and apply reading strategies

- Read pp2–9 aloud, using the meaning, dialogue and punctuation to help you read with appropriate expression.